Ask an Animal!

Ask an Animal About a Pond

Written by
Rebecca Phillips-Bartlett

WINDMILL BOOKS

Published in 2024 by Windmill Books,
an Imprint of Rosen Publishing
2544 Clinton St.
Buffalo, NY 14224

Writen by: Rebecca Phillips-Bartlett
Edited by: Elise Carraway
Designed by: Ker Ker Lee

Image Credits
All images are courtesy of Shutterstock.com, unless otherwise specified—with thanks to Getty Images, Thinkstock Photo, and iStockphoto. Frog character throughout – Olga Utchenko. Recurrring – Val_Iva, WinWin artlab, funbutterfly. Cover – Erik Steinebach. 4–5 – R. Maximiliane. 8–9 – Sasindu Bhashila, Kwangmoozaa, Wang LiQiang. 10–11 – Artur Synenko, Rostislav Stefanek Akifune. 12–13 – matthew25, Jan Miko, Rostislav Stefanek. 14–15 – R0macho, Vitalii Hulai, Kichigin. 16–17 – davemhuntphotography, Igor Klyakhin. 18–19 – stmilan, Michael Stabentheiner, sonya etchison. 20–21 – Radu Bercan, koifish. 22–23 – Shannon Jordan, Michal Dobes com.

Cataloging-in-Publication Data

Names: Phillips-Bartlett, Rebecca, 1999-.
Title: Ask an animal about a pond / Rebecca Phillips-Bartlett.
Description: Buffalo, New York: Windmill Books, 2024. | Series: Ask an animal! | Includes glossary and index.
Identifiers: ISBN 9781538291382 (pbk.) | ISBN 9781538291399 (library bound) | ISBN 9781538291405 (ebook)
Subjects: LCSH: Pond ecology--Juvenile literature. | Pond animals--Juvenile literature.
Classification: LCC QH541.5.P63 P487 2024 | DDC 577.63'6--dc23

Printed in the United States of America

CPSIA Compliance Information: Batch #CW24WM
For Further Information contact Rosen Publishing at 1-800-237-9932

Contents

Words that look like **this** can be found in the glossary on page 24.

Welcome to the Pond!

Hi! My name is Fernando. I am a frog. I am going to take you on a tour of the pond. I call the pond home, but scientists call it a habitat.

A habitat is a plant or animal's **natural** home.

Ponds might be small, but they are full of life. There is plenty to explore. On our tour, I will answer many questions you might have about life in a pond.

Pond Questions

Here are some things I am often asked about my home!

How do plants and animals **float** on top of the water?

What is a pond?

Where do tadpoles live in a pond?

As we explore, try to find the answers to these questions!

What Are Ponds?

Ponds are water habitats. They can be natural or human-made. Most ponds are small. Ponds have fresh water like lakes rather than salt water like oceans.

natural pond

human-ma pond

Have you ever visited a pond?

Ponds are important for many animals, from ducks to insects. Some animals live in ponds for their whole lives. Other animals only visit ponds to have babies or to eat.

Meet Your Guide

You probably have questions about me! Let me tell you about my life. Frogs are a type of amphibian. Amphibians are animals that can live on land and in water.

I started my life just below the **surface** of the water. Back then, I was a tiny egg. I became a tadpole, then a froglet. Now, I am a frog.

Did you know frogs breathe and drink through their skin?

On the Surface

Can you see what I am sitting on? It is a lily pad. Lily pads are water lily leaves. Water lilies have long, thick stems that connect them to the bottom of the pond.

Under the surface, water lily stems look like this.

Look at these tiny insects floating on the surface! These are water striders. They have tiny, **water-repellent** hairs on their body. These hairs let them skate on the water without falling through.

Under the Surface

Many pond animals start their lives under the water's surface. Dragonflies spend most of their lives underwater! Before they look like dragonflies, dragonfly nymphs can live underwater for up to 5 years.

dragonfly nymph

Some animals, such as snails and worms, spend their whole lives underwater. Ponds are full of plants that many animals eat. Many different types of **algae** can also be found under the water.

Around the Pond

The land around the pond is also an important part of the pond habitat. Many plants and animals live around ponds. Ponds give these animals all the food and water they need to live.

Toads live on the damp land around ponds. Like frogs, toads are amphibians. However, there are lots of differences between us. Frogs have smooth, wet skin and are great swimmers. Toads have drier, **warty** skin.

Water birds

Birds that live in and around water are waterbirds. Many waterbirds use ponds to get water, food, and shelter. Other birds, such as blackbirds, visit ponds to clean themselves.

Ducks are waterbirds. They have **webbed** feet which help them swim. People sometimes feed ducks bread. However, bread is not very good for ducks. Special food made for ducks is healthier.

Fish

Many types of freshwater fish live in ponds. Different types of fish live in different parts of the world. Many fish eat the plants and algae that grow in ponds.

How many koi can you see?

Some fish, such as goldfish, even eat tadpoles. These fish can make pond life pretty dangerous for us frogs. In the wild, goldfish also eat worms, plants, and more.

Thanks for Visiting!

Thank you for visiting my pond! I hope you enjoyed your tour. From water-walking critters to feathered friends, we have met a lot of the animals who share my pond habitat.

What is your favorite pond animal?

What do you think living in a pond would be like?

Did our dip into the pond help answer any of the questions you had about ponds? Head back to page 6, and discover how many of the questions you can answer!

Glossary

algae plantlike living things that usually grow in water and have no roots, stems, leaves, or flowers

float to rest on the surface of water without sinking

natural found in nature and not made by people

surface the outside layer of something

warty covered in small, hard lumps

water-repellent able to stop most water from coming through

webbed having toes that are connected with a flap of skin

Index